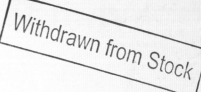

Turn it Off!

Contents

Claire Llewellyn
Character illustrations by Jon Stuart

OXFORD

What is energy?

We use energy all the time. Energy gives us light. It gives us heat and sound. Energy makes things move.

Energy makes lightbulbs work.

Energy makes cars move.

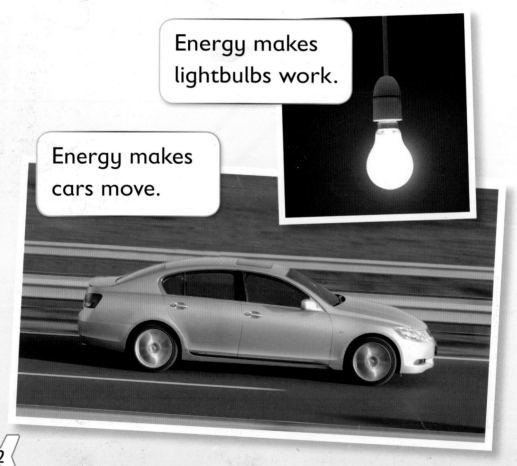

We make energy by burning **fuels** like oil, gas and **coal**.

These fuels are running out. They will last longer if we save energy.

A television uses energy.

We get energy by eating food.

Turn off the lights

Have you ever been told to turn the light off when it is not dark?

Lights need energy to make them work. If you leave the lights on when you don't need them, you **waste** energy.

Save hot water

It takes a lot of energy to heat water. Baths use a lot of hot water.

If you take a short shower, you will save water and energy.

SAVE IT!

Take a shower if you can.

Turn it off!

Machines use a lot of energy.

If you leave machines on all the time, you are wasting energy.

Top tip!
Machines can look turned off when they are still on. If a light is on, the machine is still using energy.

SAVE IT!

stereo

television

games console

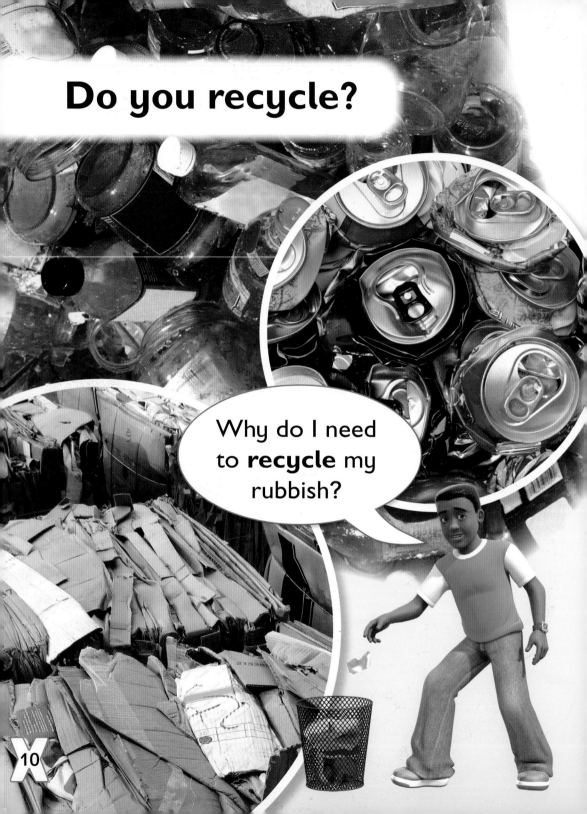

It takes a lot of energy to make paper, glass and metal. If we recycle paper, glass bottles and cans we can save energy.

SAVE IT!

Get moving

Many of us go to work or school in the car. Cars use lots of energy. This comes from burning fuel.

SAVE IT!

Some children go to school in a walking bus.

Walking, cycling or taking the bus saves fuel.

Energy quiz

1 Name three things that use energy.

2 How can we save energy in the house?

3 How can we use less hot water?

4 Why do we recycle some rubbish?

5 What kinds of rubbish can we recycle?

Glossary

coal   hard, black rock that is burned to make energy

fuel   anything that is burned to make energy

recycle   to use something again, to make rubbish into something new

waste   to use more of something than you need to

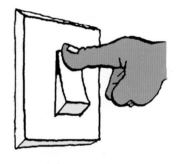

Index

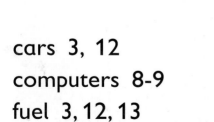

16